T010267

IT WILL STAND: LEADER'S GUIDE

IN HOME BIBLE STUDY FOR TEENS

MARY LOVE EYSTER, WEETY VICKERY

WESTBOW
PRESS
A DIVISION OF THOMAS NELSON

Copyright © 2012 by Mary Love Eyster, Weety Vickery.

All rights reserved. No part of this book may be used or reproduced by any means, graphic, electronic, or mechanical, including photocopying, recording, taping or by any information storage retrieval system without the written permission of the publisher except in the case of brief quotations embodied in critical articles and reviews.

All scripture taken from The Adventure Bible: A Study Bible for Kids. Copyright 1989 by The Zondervan Corporation.

The Holy Bible, New International Version Copyright 1973, 1978, 1984 by International Bible Society

WestBow Press books may be ordered through booksellers or by contacting:

WestBow Press
A Division of Thomas Nelson
1663 Liberty Drive
Bloomington, IN 47403
www.westbowpress.com
1-(866) 928-1240

Because of the dynamic nature of the Internet, any web addresses or links contained in this book may have changed since publication and may no longer be valid. The views expressed in this work are solely those of the author and do not necessarily reflect the views of the publisher, and the publisher hereby disclaims any responsibility for them.

Any people depicted in stock imagery provided by Thinkstock are models, and such images are being used for illustrative purposes only.

Certain stock imagery © Thinkstock.

ISBN: 978-1-4497-3191-5 (sc)
ISBN: 978-1-4497-3190-8 (e)

Library of Congress Control Number: 2011960872

Printed in the United States of America

WestBow Press rev. date: 1/12/2012

Contents

With devotion always to our spiritual leader,

John C. Eyster Sr.

Preface

Dear girls,

We live in an ever-changing world! My mother and I began in-home Bible studies for all three of my daughters when each was in the fifth grade, and they continued through high school. That was twenty years ago. We still hear how much it meant to some of our girls. I now have been teaching groups for the past eight years on my own. Isn't it amazing that the same Scriptures that were given to our ancestors are still relevant for us today? The Ten Commandments that were written on the stones and given to the Israelites impart the same instruction for us in our day-to-day living. The Scriptures are just as alive and helpful as when they were first given. I have found God's Word is like opening a treasure chest; so many pearls of wisdom await us if we only take the time to read and learn! Take a trip with me now as we discover what the Bible is "all about" and how it applies to you as an individual.

—Weety Vickery

Suggestions

To make your Bible Study successful, you may want to include some guest speakers throughout the year. Four suggested times would be:

After Lesson 13   An evangelistic speaker
After Lesson 16   A pro-life speaker
After Lesson 18   A speaker who has overcome hardship, ex: cancer survivor
After Lesson 20   A prison ministry speaker

Leader answers, optional discussion questions, and other useful topics are shown in italics.

I found many helpful video clips online that enhanced different lessons. For example: search creation, Ten Commandments, etc.

All scripture taken from The Adventure Bible: A Study Bible for Kids. Copyright 1989 by The Zondervan Corporation.

The Holy Bible, New International Version Copyright 1973, 1978, 1984 by International Bible Society

PART ONE

The Bible, What's It All About?

LESSON 1

A DIVERSE BOOK WITH A COMMON THREAD

To prepare:

- *Have computer printouts on the men in question 11.*
- *Have supplies ready and set out for the art project.*
- *Place a dictionary on the table.*

Today, work through the lesson quickly to allow time for your art project. Have Bibles available on the table, and let students take turns reading the Scriptures. (I suggest having the lesson's Scripture address already written out on a card and give to students as they sit down so they can begin looking it up.)

This might be a good time to take some pictures of the students. You will need head shots for lesson 12, and it would be fun to have pictures for a scrapbook or slide show at the end of the year!

The Bible is far and away the best-selling book of all time. It has been translated into more languages than any other book. It is the most influential book ever written.

1) Why study the Bible? II Timothy 3:16 *"All scripture is God-breathed and is useful for teaching, rebuking, correcting and training in righteousness"* I like to use a "path" to illustrate the meaning of these words. Teaching gets you on the path. Rebuke shows you that you are off the path. Correction gets you back on the path, and training in righteousness tells you how to stay on the path.

2) Why study the Bible together? Matthew 18:20 *"For where two or three come together in my name, there am I with them."* Studying together is a way to learn from each other and encourage one another.

3) What are the two divisions into which the Bible is divided? The *Old* and the *New* Testaments.

4) How many books are found in the Bible? There are *sixty-six* total. *Thirty-nine* books in the Old Testament and *twenty-seven* in the New Testament.

5) What is the span of time that separates the end of the Old Testament and the beginning of the New Testament? *It is four hundred years.*

The Bible is unique in its continuity.

Josh McDowell says, "Biblical authors spoke on hundreds of controversial subjects with harmony and continuity from Genesis to Revelation. There is one unfolding story: God's redemption of man." Josh McDowell, *Evidence that Demands a Verdict* (San Bernardino, CA: Here's Life Publishers, Inc., 1972, 1979) p 16.

Look up the word "redemption" in the dictionary. Write the meaning.

6) The Bible has some *forty* authors from many different walks of life.

7) The Bible was written over a time span of approximately *fifteen hundred* years. It was written on three continents: Asia, Africa, and Europe.

8) The original Scriptures were written in three languages: *Hebrew, Aramaic, and Greek.* Through the years, the Bible has been translated over and over again into many different languages and versions.

The Bible is unique in its circulation.

The Bible has been read by more people and published in more languages than any other book in history. No other book has known anything that approaches this constant circulation. It has been estimated that as of 2007, approximately 7.5 billion Bibles have been distributed throughout the world—not including digital versions. The complete Bible has been published in over 450 languages, the New Testament in nearly 1,400 languages. Fred R. Coulter, *The Holy Bible in Its Original Order* (Hollister, California: York Publishing Company, 2009) p 10.

According to the Gideons, Wycliffe International and the International Bible Societies it is estimated that 168,000 Bibles are bought or given out every day.

The average American household has approximately four Bibles.
How many Bibles would you estimate are in your household?

9) Many kings, emperors, rulers, and princes throughout history have tried to ban, outlaw, and destroy the Bible. Yet today, it is *the best-selling* book of all time.

10) Why do you think so many people through the years have tried to destroy or discredit the Bible? *Pause and let the students answer. The Bible has mighty power and influence to actually change lives. There will always be those who want to do things "their way" instead of God's.*

The Bible is unique in its influence.

Historian Philip Schaff wrote, "This Jesus of Nazareth, without money and arms, conquered more millions than Alexander, Caesar, Mohammed, and Napoleon; without science and learning, He shed more light on things human and divine than all philosophers and scholars combined; without the eloquence of schools. He spoke such words of life as were never spoken before or since and produced effects which lie beyond the reach of orator or poet without writing a single line. He set more pens in motion, and furnished themes for more sermons, orations, discussions, learned volumes, works of art, and songs of praise than the whole army of great men of ancient and modern times." Philip Schaff, *The Person of Christ* (New York: American Tract Society, 1913) p 33.

11) What became of some of the early men who believed in the importance of translating the Scriptures into their native languages? Some examples of these men are William Tyndale, Martin Luther, Casiodoro de Reina, and Thomas Cranmer. *(Supply computer handouts on these men for students to study and answer this question.) They were killed for their beliefs.*

The Bible's influence on these men must have been profound. They believed God's message had to be shared at any cost.

12) What did Jesus say about his "words" in Mark 13:31? *"Heaven and earth will pass away, but my words will never pass away."*

Suggest for further study that the students familiarize themselves with the books of their Bibles.

Art Project

Make wood plaques with Isaiah 40:8 "The grass withers and the flowers fall, but the word of our God stands forever."

Suggestion: Have the Scripture printed on card stock and cut to fit the size and shape of the wooden plaques. Also have paper plate palettes, newspaper, water jars, brushes, and glue set up in a separate area if possible. Have a hair dryer available for quick drying. (I let the students leave their plaques at my house to dry, and I brushed a couple of layers of protective coating on them. When dry, I used a staple gun to staple a drink pop top on the back for a hanger. Have them ready to give out at the next session. They can look at this Scripture throughout the year.)

Song of the Week: "Ancient Words" by Michael W. Smith (can be found online)

LESSON 2

SYNOPSIS OF THE BIBLE, PART I
GENESIS THROUGH EXODUS

To prepare: Have a set of Pickup Sticks (playing cards could also be used) for creation demonstration.

Familiarize yourself with the stories in this lesson so you can provide additional details. Show the students how God used different situations to bring about his purpose.

The next few lessons are a review of the *entire* Bible. You will see the common thread that is woven throughout these sixty-six books.

Genesis—the book of beginnings! We see the creation of the world and plant, animal, and human life. It is in this book that we see the origin of God's fellowship with man; the first sin; and the birth of God's chosen people, the Jews, as a nation. The primary figures of the Jewish race are Abraham, Isaac, Jacob, and Joseph.

Many other Old Testament stories are found in Genesis. See if the students can name some of them. Examples: Noah, Tower of Babel, Sodom and Gomorrah

Creation—nothing orderly comes from chaos.

At this time, share the "Pickup Sticks" demonstration. Take time to place each stick in a circle, like the rays of a sun. Gather the sticks back in your hand. Now ask the group, "How many times would I have to drop these to make them fall back into their original pattern?" God carefully made the world. A "big bang" could have never brought things together, only torn them apart!

1) The first man was named *Adam*, and his wife was *Eve*.

2) It took God *six* days to create the earth and on the *seventh* day, he rested.

God made a contract (Gen. 17:2-4) with Abram.

3) Why might we call Abraham "Father Abraham"? Genesis 17:5-6 *God tells Abraham that he will make him a "father of nations" and that he will give him millions of descendants. He also is very special because he is in the lineage of Jesus the Christ.*

4) Why was his son Isaac so special to him? Genesis 21 *Isaac was conceived by Abraham's wife, Sarah, in her old age. His other son, Ishmael, had been born by his Egyptian slave girl, Hagar.*

5) What did God ask Abraham to do with Isaac? Genesis 22 <u>*God told Abraham to sacrifice him.*</u>

Thankfully, God spared Isaac, and he later married and had a son, Jacob, and grandson, Joseph.

Has anyone heard the story of Jacob and Esau?

6) Joseph's brothers were jealous of him as a child because he was his father's favorite. Do you remember the story of the special gift his dad gave him, a coat of many colors? What did Joseph's brothers do to him? Genesis 37 *They sold him into slavery, and he was taken to Egypt. (You might expand upon the story more if time permits. Example: Joseph's dreams.)*

Family favoritism is never a good thing. It can lead to jealousy, hurt feelings, and possibly worse. Do you ever feel like your parents love your brother or sister more than you? You might ask your parents if they ever felt that way when they were young and talk about the story of Joseph.

It happened then, just as it does many times even today, that what the brothers meant for evil, God used for good. Joseph ended up forgiving his brothers, saving his family from famine, and bringing the Israelites to Egypt to live.

God could not use Joseph further without him forgiving his brothers. Do you think you could forgive such a thing if it happened to you?

Through the years, the brothers and their families grew to be a huge nation of people, and the Egyptians decided to make them slaves. They even went so far as to kill the newborn baby boys to keep the population down.

Exodus *What word does this word sound like? Exit meaning to leave.*

7) One mother went to great measures to save her baby. She hid him in a basket and floated him in the river. Who is this famous baby? Exodus 2 <u>*Moses*</u>

8) How did God place the baby Moses into Pharaoh's house to accomplish the work he later had for him? Exodus 2:1-10 *The Pharaoh's daughter found the baby Moses floating in a basket in the river when she came down to bathe. Her heart was moved, and she decided to take him back to the palace and raise him as her own.*

9) God later spoke to Moses in the burning bush and instructed him <u>*to lead the Israelites out of slavery from Egypt*</u>. (Exodus 3:6-10).

Share with the students that Moses was frightened. He even used his "lack of being able to speak in public" for an excuse.

In Exodus 3:11 Moses asked, "Who am I, that I should go to Pharaoh and bring the Israelites out of Egypt?" Don't you know he was terrified for his life and wondered how in the world the release of the Israelites could even come about? Have you ever felt that you had a task that was just too large for you to even think about tackling? God's reply in the next verse, Exodus 3:12, is one we should remember: "I will be with you."

Song of the week: "The Hope of a Broken World" by Selah

LESSON 3

Synopsis of the Bible, Part II
Leviticus through Kings

Prepare: Have students turn to the table of contents of the books of the Bible and follow along as you go through in order. A map showing the travels of the Israelites and the divided kingdom could be helpful.

This week we are going to pick up the pace a little since we only got to the second book in the Bible last week! We take right back up with the Israelite nation. They have left a life of slavery in Egypt and are establishing their new life in a new land.

Leviticus: God sets up the laws, sacrificial system, priesthood, and special feasts that were to be celebrated during the year. Henrietta Mears said, "One of the most important questions in life is 'How may an unholy people approach a holy God?'" Henrietta Mears, *What the Bible is All About* (Venture, CA: Regal Books, 1983) p 52. At the very beginning of the book, we see God making provision for his people to approach him in worship. Sin is no small matter, and dealing with it is of great importance to God. Take time now to read Leviticus 1. *Warning, this can be gory!*

Numbers: This book is simple enough; the Israelites are numbered. They entered Egypt a family of seventy and exited 430 years later a nation of some six hundred thousand men twenty years old and older, plus women and children, an estimated total of some two to three million people. These people murmured and complained and rebelled against God and as a result failed to enter the promised land of Canaan at their first opportunity. They learned the hard lesson that punishment follows disobedience. It took them forty years to make an eleven-day journey.

Punishment followed disobedience. Is this still true today? Think of examples.

Moses was not without punishment himself. In Numbers 20, God instructed him to speak to a rock so that it would pour out water. Moses did not follow God's instructions. He struck the rock instead, and therefore he was not allowed to enter the Promised Land. Does this punishment seem a bit severe to you? Does it show us how serious God is about sin?

Deuteronomy: This word means "repetition of the law." At the end of their long journey, the Israelites were ready to enter Canaan, the land that God had promised to Abraham and his descendents. Moses was about to die, so he gave final instructions to the people he had guided for the forty years. He reminded them to obey God.

The next twelve books are history books, telling of the major events in the nation of Israel.

Remember the song, "Joshua Fought the Battle of Jericho"?

Joshua: This book tells how the Israelites entered the Promised Land and conquered it under the leadership of Joshua, Moses's successor. In Numbers 13 and 14, Moses sent spies into Canaan. Read Numbers 14:1-9 to see why Joshua was such a good choice as the Israelites' new leader. God had given them the land, but they had to possess their new possession. This is true in the spiritual realm as well. God has given us all great and wonderful promises, but we must claim them and live by them for them to become truly ours.

Treasure Chest Story

A man went to heaven and was shown a calendar of all the days of his life. On most of the days, there were unopened treasure chests. When the man asked what they were, God explained that they were treasures that were there for his taking. He just hadn't received them. How often are we so busy that we don't look for or receive the gifts (treasures) that God desires to freely give us?

Judges: The book of Judges tells how the Israelites would fall into disobedience and idolatry, and God would give them over to their enemies. Then the people would cry out to God, and God would send them a leader, called a judge, to rescue them. This cycle occurred seven times. The last verse in the book of Judges, 21:25, gives a sad summary of this book: "In those days Israel had no king; everyone did as he saw fit."

- What happens to a group of people with no leader or a weak leader?
- Does that sound like contemporary philosophy?
- Do you think people tend to draw closer to God or think more spiritually after a major catastrophe and then fall away again when times are better? *An example of this was the 9/11 tragedy.*

These questions are for thought and discussion. Just like the ancient Israelites, we tend to earnestly worship God at times and then fall away. A great pastor, a group leader, a Christian retreat, or sadly even a tragedy can tend to make us draw close to God. It is regrettable that we have to have outside influence to help us stay focused.

Ruth: The sweet story of the young woman named Ruth tells of her faith in the God of her mother-in-law, Naomi. Naomi helped Ruth "date" and then she won the heart of Boaz, a most eligible bachelor. Ruth later married Boaz. He became the father of Obed, the grandfather of Jesse, and the great grandfather of King David. This placed Ruth in the ancestral line of Christ.

I Samuel: This begins the five hundred-year period of the kings of Israel. In 1 Samuel the Israelites asked God for a king like the other nations had. God was not pleased but granted their request and gave them Saul. The book of 1 Samuel covers a period of about 115 years. It begins with the childhood of Samuel and runs through Saul's kingship and then into the beginning of the reign of King David. Samuel was the last of the judges, and Saul was the first of the kings. Second Samuel tells us how David became Saul's successor on the throne. David was a mighty warrior and a wise king. The kingdom was expanded, and the nation was highly unified under David's rule. *What do you remember about David? He was a shepherd boy. He played a harp. He fought the giant Goliath. He wrote many Psalms. He sinned with Bathsheba and was later called "a man after God's own heart."*

Why do you think it displeased God so much when the Israelites insisted on having a king? *They wanted to be like the other nations. Oftentimes we get in trouble when we desire to copy others. God wanted them to depend upon him alone.*

King David's son was Solomon. What do you remember about him? In 1 Kings 3:5 God granted Solomon anything he would like. Do you know what he requested? Let the students read down from 1 Kings 3:5 and discover that he asked for wisdom!

I Kings: At King David's death, we see his son Solomon rise to the throne. He built the first temple, which was a large, elaborately decorated building. He had very specific building instructions from God (1 Kings 6). Solomon was known for his wisdom, but later in his life, he sought poor advice from friends and did not listen to God. His choice to do this actually changed the history of Israel. After his death, the kingdom divided under two leaders, Jeroboam and Rehoboam. It split into the northern kingdom, or Israel, and the southern kingdom, or Judah. II Kings gives us some of the history of the different kings of the two kingdoms. The southern kingdom (Judah) had twenty kings, and the northern kingdom (Israel) had nineteen kings. Some of Judah's leaders were godly and some wicked. All of the kings of Israel were wicked; none led their subjects to worship the true God. Henrietta Mears said, "During Solomon's reign the kingdom reached the height of its grandeur. With the death of Solomon, the kingship really ceased to be the medium through which God governed His people. The decline of the kingdoms is portrayed until we see both Israel and Judah led into captivity." Henrietta Mears, *What the Bible is All About* (Venture, CA:

Regal Books, 1983) p 136. The Assyrians captured the Northern Kingdom in 722 BC, and the Southern Kingdom fell to the Babylonians around 586 BC.

In 1 Kings 2:1-4, David is about to die and gives a charge to his son. This is advice he wants his son to remember. What did David say?

Have you ever thought about what would be your last most important words to a loved one?

Song of the week: "You Reign" by Mercy Me

LESSON 4

SYNOPSIS OF THE BIBLE, PART III
I CHRONICLES THROUGH SONG OF SOLOMON

Prepare: Have a map of the split kingdoms, and their captors. Provide magazines for students to look through.

I Chronicles: This book gives us some history parallel to that of II Samuel. It begins with the death of Saul, gives many details about the reign of David, and ends with David's death.

II Chronicles parallels 1 Kings, with Solomon's reign and the division of the kingdom. It goes further to tell about the succeeding kings in both Israel and Judah.

Show the map.

Both the Assyrians and Babylonians carried Israelites away captive. The captives from Israel never returned from exile in Assyria. Some of the captives from Judah did return from exile in Babylon to rebuild the temple, its walls, and the city of Jerusalem, which had been destroyed by the Babylonians.

Ezra and Nehemiah: These two books tell of the return of the captives and the restoration of the temple and Jerusalem under the rule of the Persians who conquered the Babylonians. The time covered by these two books is approximately a hundred years.

What if your home land was destroyed by war or a natural disaster? Do you think you would return to repair and rebuild?

Esther: In 479 BC Esther became the queen of Persia when she became the wife of Xerxes. God placed Esther in the palace to preserve the Jewish nation from extinction. God had great plans for his chosen people. He intended to bless the whole world through them, and he did so by sending the Messiah and giving the world the Scriptures and the belief in one God through the Jews.

Just like there was a special God-appointed time, place, and purpose for Esther in history, there is also one for you!

You might like to share more of the story of Queen Esther and her famous line in Esther 4:16, "And if I perish, I perish."

The Poetry Books
Job, Psalms, Proverbs, Ecclesiastes, and Song of Solomon

Ask the students, "Who has heard of Job and his story?" Briefly describe it. God allows suffering in our lives so his glory can be revealed through us.

Job: This is considered the oldest book of the Bible, and it deals with one of the oldest problems: why do bad things happen to good people? People have always been perplexed and frustrated when God permits his faithful to suffer. This book takes you through many stages of Job's suffering. Think of how faithful Job was to God. He did not have Scripture to guide him, yet he offered sacrifices to God on behalf of his children. He also remained faithful through his bodily suffering and the rejection of God by his wife and friends!

In chapters 37-42, God reminds Job of his greatness! Who are we to question what he is doing? You might want to read some of this.

God uses trials and suffering in our lives many different ways. Can you think of some? Would anyone like to share a personal example?

Psalms: The Hebrew title of Psalms is "Praise" or the "Book of Praises," and the main content of this book is praise, prayer, and worship. The Psalms were like the national hymnal of Israel. They contain 150 poems to be sung to music. These poems run through a full range of human emotion: joy, sorrow, victory, failure, trust, fear, and pleas for help. Each scripture should be considered with its context.

Proverbs: Here we find wise counsel for everyday living.

There are thirty-one chapters in Proverbs. This book makes a wonderful daily devotional since there is one chapter for each day of the month.

Ecclesiastes: Solomon tells of his search for meaning, purpose, and happiness in life. He tried it all, saying that everything but *knowing God* is a dead end. It's useless, meaningless, and could be considered vanity in the long run. He gives his conclusion in Ecclesiastes 12:13: "Fear God, and keep his commandments: for this is the whole duty of man."

What are some things people use today to fill their lives with happiness and meaning? Do these things truly fulfill? For how long?

Teacher: Provide teen and fashion magazines for the students to look through.

Song of Solomon: The Song of Solomon has been called the Christian's love song. The love between a man and a woman in this book gives us a picture of the love between God and his people. The greatest commandment is for us to love God with all our heart, soul, mind, and strength. We are challenged to such wholehearted devotion in the Song of Solomon.

Today's study has given us another history lesson but also introduced us to the beautiful poetry books. They encourage us during our suffering and help us overcome adversity. They give us hymns of praise and verses of wise counsel. Man has always searched for the meaning of life, and I love the way Solomon puts it—everything but knowing God is useless!

Song of the Week: "Word of God Speak" by Mercy Me

LESSON 5

Synopsis of the Bible, Part IV
Prophecy Books Through the New Testament

This is the final lesson in our walk through the Bible. Hopefully it will give you an overall view of what the Bible encompasses.

Prepare: Show a map of the divided kingdoms.

The seventeen prophetic books in the Old Testament are divided into two categories: the Major Prophets, of which there are five; and the Minor Prophets, of which there are twelve. The messages of the Minor Prophets are not necessarily less important than the messages of the Major Prophets, but the books are shorter!

Remember how faithful and caring God has been to his people. He led them out of captivity and through the Red Sea. He gave them the ten commandments to guide them. Instead of reverencing and obeying God, the Israelite people chose to do their own thing and not listen to God's instructions. At this time, God raised up prophets to lead the people. These prophets spoke courageously to kings and common people alike. They not only addressed sins and failures but also gave promises of God's comfort.

Who today would you liken to the Old Testament prophets?

Let's take a look at *Daniel,* one of the more familiar prophets. Read Daniel 9 to see an example of a prophet's job.

After the last voice of the prophets died out, there were four hundred years of silence from God to man before the birth of Jesus. In other words, there were four hundred years between the Old and New Testaments.

Remember the Northern Kingdom, or Israel, was conquered by the Assyrians around 722 BC, and many of the people were carried into exile. The Southern Kingdom, or Judah, was conquered by the Babylonians around 586 BC, and many of the Jews were taken into exile.

17

The prophets can be divided into those who prophesied to Israel and those who prophesied to Judah. They can also be divided into those who prophesied before part of the Jewish nation was taken captive into exile, those who prophesied during the exile, and those who prophesied after the exile.

Have students continue to locate the following books in their Bible as you go through the lesson.

The prophets to Israel before their exile were Jonah, Amos, and Hosea. The prophets to Judah before their exile were Obadiah, Joel, Isaiah, Micah, Nahum, Habakkuk, Zephaniah, and Jeremiah.

The prophets during the exile or captivity in Babylon were Ezekiel and Daniel. Jeremiah extended partially into this period as well.

Those who prophesied to Judah after the exile were Haggai, Zechariah, and Malachi.

Prophets were never sent when a nation was walking in obedience to God. They were always sent to warn the people that God was displeased with them and tell them what would happen if they continued down the wrong road. Not only did the prophets speak of judgment to come, but they often foretold future events as well.

New Testament

God loved his children so much that he went to all kinds of measures to communicate with them. How would you have communicated if there were no phones, computers, or TVs? You might have written a letter. God wrote us a beautiful love letter. It is the Bible. He communicated through prophets, angels, burning bushes, dreams, and natural phenomena. Now he is about to make the boldest move of all. He is actually coming to earth to try to woo us to himself in person! He is a pursuer God.

The Gospels
Matthew, Mark, Luke, and John

These are actual first-hand accounts from men who walked and talked with Jesus. They were from different walks of life. Matthew was a tax collector. Mark's occupation was not given. Luke was a doctor. John was a fisherman. They all had very different backgrounds and education. This made their accounts of the same event unique.

Matthew: Was written primarily to the Jews and contains a number of Scriptures that show how Jesus fulfilled some of the Old Testament prophecies.

Mark: Was written primarily for the Romans, who were men of action. It is fast moving and tells more of what Jesus did than what he said.

Luke: Was primarily written to the Gentiles. It has a more universal appeal.

John: Was written so that whoever reads this book may conclude that Jesus is the Christ, the Son of God. John concentrated on Jesus's miracles and explained the meanings behind them.

The remainder of the New Testament contains the following:

Acts: A history book. This book tells of Pentecost and the early days of the church.

Romans, 1 & 2 Corinthians, Galatians, Ephesians, Philippians, Colossians, 1 & 2 Thessalonians, 1 & 2 Timothy, Titus, Philemon, Hebrews, James, 1 & 2 Peter, 1, 2 & 3 John, and Jude: These books include twenty-one epistles (letters), fourteen of which were written by Paul. Many were written to instruct and encourage the new churches that were started as a result of the impact that Jesus' life had upon the earth.

Revelation: The book of the future. This book is John's "vision into heaven." It is a prophetic view of what is to come. God and Satan will have their last "showdown." One day Christ will return to gather his believers. Some refer to this as the rapture. After Christ's return, the Bible tells us that there will be a time of tremendous suffering for the people left on earth. Those who are unbelievers will have a time period to turn to the Lord and be saved. Revelation also gives us a glimpse of all the wonderful things that await believers in heaven. At this time, read Revelation 22.

- The Old Testament tells us to "get ready" because someone is coming.
- The Gospels tell us, "He is here."
- Revelation tells us, "He is coming again."

The book of Revelation tells us that Jesus Christ will one day return as King of kings and Lord of lords to reign forever. He is coming back to receive his church. Won't it be exciting to be a part of his story!

Song of the Week: "When the Saints Go Marching In" by Sara Groves

LESSON 6

How Do We Know That the Bible Is Really God's Word?

Do you believe that the Bible is true? Is it trustworthy? Is it believable?

The purpose of this lesson is to show the students that the Bible has stood the test of time. The same instructions given to the early Israelites are true for us today. This lesson introduces the Ten Commandments! It is very important that the students learn them in order. Give out a keepsake of some kind with the commandments printed on it for them to take.

We have already seen that the Bible is a unique book. No other book could possess the characteristics and the history that the Bible contains without having been written by the hand of God. Think about it . . .

The Bible is unique in its *continuity*. We learned that the Bible was written over a time span of fourteen hundred to sixteen hundred years by approximately forty authors from many different walks of life. It was written on three continents and in three languages, yet there is harmony and agreement throughout. The Bible tells one story from beginning to end.

The Bible is unique in its *circulation*. It is, far and away, the best seller of all time. No other book has approached its number of copies—printed or read.

The Bible is unique in its *survival*. It has survived being tediously copied by hand many times with remarkable accuracy. It has also survived criticism, skepticism, and persecution.

It never goes out of date. Share with the students some "fad" words that you used that are now outdated.

The Bible is more than just *unique*. It claims to be written by God himself.

Look up these Scriptures:

- 2 Peter 1:20-21: *"Above all, you must understand that no prophecy of Scripture came about by the prophet's own interpretation. For prophecy never had its origin in the will of man, but men spoke from God as they were carried along by the Holy Spirit."*

- 2 Timothy 3:16: *"All scripture is God-breathed and is useful for teaching, for rebuking, correcting and training in righteousness."*

In the production of Scripture, both God and man were active participants. God worked through human authors to give us his words. The writings were colored by the unique personalities and circumstances of each individual writer, but God caused each one to write what he wanted. This is what is meant when you hear that Scripture is the *inspired* Word of God.

A. The Old Testament asserts that its writings are from God. Over two thousand examples are found, and the following are just a few:

- Isaiah 1:2b: *"The Lord has spoken"*
- Ezekiel 6:1: *"The word of the Lord came to me"*
- Hosea 4:1: *"Hear the word of the Lord"*
- Amos 1:3: *"This is what the Lord says"*

B. New Testament writers believed that their words were inspired by God as well. Paul wrote to the Thessalonians, "And we also thank God continually because, when you received the word of God, which you heard from us, you accepted it not as the word of men, but as it actually is, the word of God, which is at work in you who believe" (1 Thessalonians 2:13).

Paul also wrote in 1 Corinthians 2:13, *"This is what we speak, not in words taught us by human wisdom but in words taught by the spirit, expressing spiritual truths in spiritual words."*

C. Jesus recognized the Old Testament as being from God and quoted it on numerous occasions. Matthew 5:17-18, Deuteronomy 8:3, Matthew 19:4-5.

Jesus believed that the entire Old Testament was the Word of God. If we believe Jesus, we will believe the Bible. Further, if we believe the Bible, we should believe Jesus. This belief is fundamental to the doctrine of the Christian faith.

How can we understand the Bible? The Holy Spirit is the one who guides us in understanding and applying God's Word. I Corinthians 2:11-12 says, "For who among men knows the thoughts of a man except the man's spirit within him? In the same way no one knows the thoughts of God except the Spirit of God. We have not received the spirit of the world but the Spirit who is from God, that we may understand what God has freely given us."

Who has the Holy Spirit living in them to give this understanding? It is the people who acknowledge that they are sinners and cannot do anything to make themselves pure before a Holy God. They accept that Jesus Christ has died on the cross to pay the penalty for their sins. They receive God's complete forgiveness and now have Jesus' righteousness imputed to them. (In other words, when God looks at them, he sees people with a clean record!) They are now beloved, adopted children of God. They are filled with the Holy Spirit who will never, ever leave them!

Do you believe that all Scripture is true for all people all of the time? For example:

1) Is it okay to be dishonest sometimes?
2) Is it okay to cheat on a test if everyone is doing it?
3) Is it okay to make fun of your mother to your friends?
4) Is it okay to use God's name without respect?

How about stealing, jealousy, and adultery?

There are two ways to look at the world: a biblical way and a non-biblical way.

Proverbs 14:12 says, "There is a way that seems right to a man, but in the end it leads to death." This verse is true today. We have access to more knowledge than ever before but seem to be lacking wisdom, especially biblical wisdom.

Many people want to live in a way that seems right to *them,* not by the teachings of the *Bible.* Many will argue that we should be "tolerant" of other people's beliefs and claim that what is right or wrong for you might not be right or wrong for me.

There is a body of absolute truth, truth that is true in every situation, and this body of truth is found in the Bible. Scripture gives us the truth about God, about creation including mankind, about sin and salvation, and about the eternal future of each person.

I love the fact that the same Ten Commandments that God gave to Moses some thirty-five hundred years ago are still relevant today. The sinful heart of man is basically facing the same old problems that it faced in biblical times and has dealt with ever since.

Have each student try to list the Ten Commandments. Tell them to list them in order if they can. Later, after you go over them, ask if anyone got them all correct.

The Ten Commandments
Exodus 20

1) I am the Lord your God. You shall have no other God's before me.

2) You shall not make for yourself an idol.

3) You shall not misuse the name of the Lord your God.

4) Remember the Sabbath day by keeping it holy.

5) Honor your father and your mother.

6) You shall not murder.

7) You shall not commit adultery.

8) You shall not steal.

9) You shall not give false testimony.

10) You shall not covet.

Discuss what each commandment means.

What do you notice about the ordering of the commandments?

They are ordered by importance, with God first and the ones that deal with man last.

Only God could provide us with these "living" rules that have instructed the action and touched the heart of man for centuries. Take the time to memorize these to use as a guide for yourself and also as a wonderful tool for sharing with others.

Song of the week: "The Word" by Sara Groves

LESSON 7

How Was the Bible Made, and How Do We Know it is Reliable?

Prepare: Have a dictionary available

The Bible is a story of dedication to painstaking detail. How often do we neglect to recognize and remember the thousands of years of sacrificial effort that went into the Bible that we so easily take for granted today?

A. Jewish scholars, called Talmudists, were designated to copy the Scriptures. The copyist had to wash his whole body and sit in full Jewish dress to copy a manuscript.

B. A synagogue roll had to be written on the skins of clean animals that had been prepared for the special task.

C. The ink was to be black only and prepared by a particular recipe.

D. The transcriber had to copy from an authenticated manuscript and was not to deviate in the least.

E. No word or letter, not even a yod (punctuation mark), was to be written from memory, but the scribe had to look at each one individually as he copied.

F. Between every consonant, there had to be the space of a hair or a thread. Between every new section, there had to be the breadth of nine consonants. Between every book, there was to be the space of three lines.

G. The copyists were so particular with the manuscripts that they counted the number of verses, the number of words, and the number of letters in each book. They found the middle letter of each page and each book. They even knew the middle letter of the Pentateuch and of the whole Old Testament. They carefully checked all copies by comparing the numbers of verses, words, and letters and the middle letters to see if they all matched.

Old Testament

The Pentateuch (the first five books in the Bible) is called the Law of Moses. Jesus referred to these books as being authored by Moses. How could Moses have known about the creation of the world?

1. God could have supernaturally given Moses this information, or
2. This information could have been passed down orally from generation to generation until people began to write things down.

Have you asked your parents to tell you stories? Did you have your favorites that you wanted to hear over and over again?

There was written language before Moses lived, so there could have been some written accounts of creation. Before written language, there were cave drawings. Moses could have had access to both written and oral accounts of the creation when he wrote Genesis.

What are some of the ways the Old Testament books might have been given by God to be written and preserved?

1) Moses _wrote down_ what God told him to.
2) God spoke to and _through the prophets_ who preceded their writings with such sayings as, "Thus saith the Lord."
3) Some of the books tell the story of the events of the Jews. They are _historic accounts._
4) The _psalms_ were the hymns of the Jewish nation.

Jesus himself referred to the Old Testament *canon* in Luke 24:44 when he told the disciples in the upper room, "Everything must be fulfilled, that is written about me in the Law of Moses, the Prophets and the Psalms." These were the three sections in which the Hebrew Bible was divided. Jesus quoted or made reference to thirty-five Old Testament books, confirming that he accepted them.

Look up and write the meaning of the word "canon."

The canon is an authoritative list of books accepted as Holy Scripture.

What are the books of the *Apocrypha?*

The Apocrypha are books included in the Septuagint and Vulgate but excluded from the Jewish and Protestant canons of the Old Testament, or early Christian writings not included in the New Testament.

Many other spiritual writings appeared on the scene. The Jews were careful to define which books would be included in the canon, the accepted Word of God.

New Testament

The acceptance of the books of the New Testament was a little different from the books of the Old Testament. The first-century Christians actually recorded the words of Jesus and of the apostles. The New Testament books were either written by eyewitnesses to Jesus' ministry or by those who heard firsthand these eyewitness reports.

Canonicity is *determined or fixed* by God; it is merely *discovered* by man. There were several guidelines for including a book in the New Testament canon.

1) Were the writers reliable? Was a book written by an apostle or someone who knew an apostle well and had heard him speak often?
2) Was the content reliable? Did it agree with the rest of Scripture? Did it have a sense of divine authority?
3) Was it read and used by the people of God? The accepted books were circulated through the churches and read publicly.
4) How did the early church fathers regard these books?

Josephus, the Jewish historian, wrote this at the end of the first century AD: "And how firmly we have given credit to those books of our own nation is evident by what we do: for during so many ages as have already passed, no one has been so bold as either to add anything to them or take anything from them or to make any change in them: but it becomes natural to all Jews, immediately and from their very birth, to esteem those books to contain divine doctrines, and to persist in time, and, if occasion be, willingly to die for them." Flavius Josephus, "Flavius Josephus Against Apion." *Josephus, Complete Works.* Translated by William Whiston, Grand Rapids, OR: Kregel Publications, 1960) p 609.

Athanasius of Alexandria (AD 367) gives us the earliest list of New Testament books that is exactly like our present New Testament in a letter to the churches.

F. F. Bruce states, "When at last a Church Council—the Synod of Hippo in A.D. 393—listed the 27 books of the New Testament, it did not confer upon them any authority which they did not already possess, but simply recorded their previously established canonicity." F.F. Bruce, *The Books and the Parchments*, Rev. ed. (Westwood, NJ: Fleming H. Revell Co., 1963) p 97.

Josh McDowell concludes, "Since this time, there has been no serious questioning of the 27 accepted books of the New Testament." Josh McDowell, *Evidence that Demands a Verdict* (San Bernardino, CA: Here's Life Publishers, Inc., 1972, 1979) p 38.

You can imagine how scarce and expensive copies of the Bible before the invention of the printing press would be. Very few people had Bibles in their homes. How many Bibles would you estimate you have in your home? Do you realize what a privilege it is to have instant access to the very Word of God? Are we taking full advantage of this opportunity?

A wonderful way to prove the authenticity of the Bible is to study the prophecies that were predicted and study the way in which they were fulfilled. Fulfilled prophecy is one way to see God's absolute authority and understand he is in control over the actions of heaven and earth.

What are some different methods used today to predict what is going to happen in the future? *Some methods are fortune tellers, fortune cookies, horoscopes, and weathermen.*

How accurate are their outcomes? *They are sometimes accurate, not always.*

The test of a true biblical prophet is that **all** of his predictions have to come true! He must be 100 percent correct to be a true prophet of God. In other words, there must be divine guidance and no room for human error.

The Bible contains hundreds of detailed prophecies which have been fulfilled.

You can be confident when you read your Bible that it is the inspired Word of God. It has been proven over and over, not only by fulfilled prophesies, but also by its ability to change men's hearts. I Thessalonians 2:13 says it best: "And we also thank God continually because, when you received the word of God, which you heard from us, you accepted it not as the word of men, but as it actually is, the word of God, which is at work in you who believe."

Song of the Week: "Thy Word" by Amy Grant

LESSON 8

JESUS, THE CENTERPIECE OF THE WORD

Suppose a man were to walk in here right now and claim to be God in human form. Would you believe him? Don't you think we would ask him for proof? After all, in this era of identity theft, our credentials that prove who we are have become very important, and we are required to tell or show them on certain occasions.

What are some credentials that can be shown to prove who you are? *A few are a driver's license, passport, birth certificate, or credit card.*

When God sent Jesus into the world, he knew people would be very skeptical. After all, nothing like this had ever happened before. He wanted people to recognize Jesus as who he really was, God in the flesh, so God gave Jesus some important credentials that would authenticate his claim. Think about it—if God became man, what credentials do you think he should have? What would we expect him to be like?

If *God became a man*, we would expect his birth to be different. Jesus' birth was unusual. What was "not the norm" concerning Jesus' birth? *An angel announced his birth. He was born to a virgin. He was born in a stable, etc. You would think that God would arrive in a very kingly fashion instead of in such a humble way.*

If *God became a man*, we would expect him to be without sin, to be morally perfect.

What did Pilate say about Jesus at his trial? Luke 23:4 *"I find no basis for a charge against this man."*

Read Matthew 27:3-5. What did Judas say about Jesus? *"I betrayed innocent blood."*

Read 1 Peter 2:22. Peter said, *"He committed no sin."*

When Jesus asked his enemies what sin he had committed, they were unable to name a single one.

If *God became a man,* we would expect him to have an acute sense of his difference from others.

Remember the twelve-year-old boy Jesus when he accompanied his parents to the temple in Jerusalem and stayed behind? When his parents questioned him, Jesus said, "Didn't you know I had to be in my Father's house?" Luke 2:49.

Jesus claimed to be God a number of times and in different ways.

1) Matthew 26:53 *"Do you think I cannot call on my Father, and he will at once put at my disposal more than twelve legions of angels?"*
2) John 14:9 *"Anyone who has seen me has seen the father."*

Jesus claimed to forgive sins, a privilege of God alone. Jesus claimed to be the judge of all men. Jesus asked men to put their eternal destiny in his hands.

Jesus very clearly claimed to be deity. Mark 14:61b-62 *"Again the high priest asked him, "Are you the Christ, the Son of the Blessed One?" "I am," said Jesus. "And you will see the Son of Man sitting at the right hand of the Mighty One and coming on the clouds of heaven.""*

Jesus made his claims so clear that his enemies understood them.

How did his enemies react to his claims?

John 5:18 *"For this reason the Jews tried all the harder to kill him; not only was he breaking the Sabbath, but he was even calling God his own Father, making himself equal with God."*

John 10:36 *"What about the one whom the Father set apart as his very own and sent into the world? Why then do you accuse me of blasphemy because I said, "I am God's Son?""*

If *God became a man,* we would expect other people to recognize him as divine.

In John 1:45, Philip declared, *"We have found the one Moses wrote about in the Law, and about whom the prophets also wrote—Jesus of Nazareth, the son of Joseph."*

In John 1:49, Nathanael declared, *"Rabbi, you are the Son of God; you are the King of Israel."*

In John 11:27, Martha answered, *"I believe that you are the Christ, the Son of God, who was to come into the world."*

And when Thomas saw Jesus for himself after the resurrection, he called Jesus, "my Lord and my God." John 20:28

These people knew Jesus well. But maybe Jesus' friends were prejudiced. What did others say about him?

In Luke 23:41, the repentant thief on the cross said, *"We are punished justly, for we are getting what our deeds deserve. But this man has done nothing wrong."*

In Luke 23:47, the centurion who was in charge of the crucifixion said, *"Surely this was a righteous man!"*

If *God became man,* we would expect him to perform miracles, and Jesus certainly did that.

If *God became man,* we would expect him to speak the greatest words ever spoken.

Luke 4:22 *"All spoke well of him and were amazed at the gracious words that came from his lips. "Isn't this Joseph's son?" they asked.*

John 7:46 "No one ever spoke the way this man does," the guards declared.

In John 6:68, Simon Peter answered him, *"Lord, to whom shall we go? You have the words of eternal life."*

If *God became man,* we would surely expect him to have a lasting influence on mankind.

From the essay entitled "One Solitary Life," we find these words, "Nineteen long centuries have come and gone, and today He is the centerpiece of the human race and the leader of the column of progress. I am far within the mark when I say that all the armies that ever marched, all the navies that ever were built, all the parliaments that ever sat, and all the kings that ever reigned, put together, have not affected the life of man upon this earth as powerfully as has that one solitary life." Dr. James Allan Francis, "Arise Sir Knight!" *The Real Jesus and Other Sermons* (Philadelphia, PA: The Judson Press of Philadelphia, 1926) pp 123-124.

Many still do not want to acknowledge Jesus as the Son of God, the Messiah, and the Savior of the World. They will say he was just a "good man" or a "great teacher." This is not possible because he claimed to be the Son of God. If he was just a good man or a great teacher, he would now be a liar because he said on many occasions that he was God's son. There was no room for compromise.

Song of the week: "Above All" by Michael W. Smith

PART TWO

The Bible, What Does It Mean to Me?

LESSON 9

My Personal Journey of Faith

We have spent the past eight lessons examining the authorship, structure, and authenticity of the Bible. Now it is time for application. What significance does all of this have for you personally?

Before we see where this information will lead you, let's see where you have been. Where did your spiritual journey begin? What has helped shape your faith? You are all probably at different levels of spiritual maturity. No doubt some of you are very devoted to your heavenly father and are walking closely day by day. Others may still have many questions. Some of you may not have made a commitment to God at all.

Much of the Bible is devoted to genealogy. Let's take a look and see where some of your heritage lies. Fill in the names and give one or two traits for each person on your family tree.

YOUR NAME

FATHER

MOTHER

FATHER'S PARENTS

MOTHER'S PARENTS

Like it or not, not only is eye color passed down through family lines. Actions can be passed down as well. The Bible confirms this:

- Nehemiah 1:6b *"I confess the sins we Israelites, including myself and my father's house, have committed against you."*

- Nehemiah 9:2 *"Those of Israelite decent had separated themselves from all foreigners. They stood in their places and confessed their sins and the wickedness of their fathers."*
- Ezekiel 18:14 *"But suppose this son has a son who sees all the sins his father commits, and though he sees them, he does not do such things:"*
- Psalm 79:8 *"Do not hold against us the sins of the fathers; may your mercy come quickly to meet us, for we are in desperate need."*
- Jeremiah 32:18a *"You show love to thousands but bring the punishment for the fathers' sins into the laps of their children after them."*

Good and bad traits are passed down from grandparents and parents to their children. For example, it has been noted that many times when people are abused, they often later become abusers.

Discuss with the students some other things that might have negative effects on the entire family (e.g., pornography, adultery, alcohol, gambling). Help students realize that every family has some "skeletons" in the closet. I have had students in the past who have had only one parent in their lives. I told the students that they should be thankful to that parent for the gift of life if nothing else. This seemed to bring some comfort.

If you have had some "undesirable traits" passed down to you, don't despair. God is in the life changing business. The chain *can* be broken! One reason you are here is to learn and apply the attributes of Godly behavior.

Spiritual Training

Record church affiliations, Sunday school, VBS, and other spiritual training you have had.

_____

_____

Record the names of people who have had a positive impact on your life.

_____

_____

Record a favorite childhood memory.

_____

_____

Read Psalm 139:13-18. God knew the day you were born, just as he knows exactly when he will call you to your heavenly home. Your childhood is no surprise to him. He can use the good and the bad events of your past. He never wastes an opportunity to help you grow!

Take this time to write a letter to God. Just be honest with him; he already knows your heart. You might want to thank him for your family history, the good and the bad. You might want to thank him for the opportunities he has presented to you. You might ask for his wisdom and guidance in studying his Word and tell him of your desire to know him more!

Give students ample time to do this exercise.

Have students Google popular Christian author, Josh McDowell and read his testimony. *(He grew up with an alcoholic father. He was filled with hate for his father and God and set out to disprove the Bible. The summation of information that he collected and the biblical "facts" that he could not ignore brought him to a saving knowledge of Christ.)*

Song of the week: "My Life Is in Your Hands" by Kirk Franklin

LESSON 10

EARLY EXAMPLES OF FAITH

In our last lesson, we talked about different traits we have—good and bad, inherited and learned. You wrote a letter to God expressing your desire to know him more. Do you really believe that "his ways" will make your life better, more fulfilled, and successful? Remember the Israelites? When they did things God's way, there was no need for prophets to intervene, but when they sinned, they suffered the consequences.

Since we cannot see God with our eyes at this time, we must believe or have faith with our minds and hearts. That is what today's lesson is about.

A good starting point would be Hebrews 11, also known as the faith chapter.

1. Hebrews 11:1 gives us a definition of *faith.* The Living Bible, Tyndale Publishing, translates like this: "It is the confident assurance that something we want is going to happen. It is the certainty that what we hope for is waiting for us, even though we cannot see it up ahead."
2. What do the words confident, assurance, and certainty convey to you? *They imply that it will happen, a bold belief, without a doubt, unafraid, positive, and fearless.*
3. What evidence of God does Hebrew 11:3 reveal? *"By faith we understand that the universe was formed at God's command, so that what is seen was not made out of what was visible." We are his creations.* Psalm 19:1-4 expands on this. Read it.
4. Do "all men, women, and children for all times" have access to this evidence? *Yes, even in the most remote corners of the world. We all can look and see the amazing stars, the beautiful mountains, and the vast seas and know that man could not create these.*

In Hebrews 11:4 we see the beginning of the "roll call" of the faithful.

5. Who is the first person mentioned in Hebrews 11:4? *Abel.*
6. In verse 5, what amazing reward did Enoch receive for his faithfulness? *He was taken into heaven without dying.*

7. Verse 6 shares a very important truth with us. What is it? *Without faith, it is impossible to please God.*

8. Who are the faithful mentioned in verses 7 through 12, and how did they demonstrate their faith?

   - *Noah—Listened to God and built the ark.*
   - *Abraham—Listened to God and obeyed by leaving his home to live in a country that God promised to give him.*
   - *Isaac and Jacob—Abraham's son and grandson received the same promise as Abraham did.*
   - *Abraham and his wife Sarah—They were too old to have children and Sarah was barren, but God gave them a son.*

9. Verses 13 through 16 reveal something about the people of faith previously mentioned. What is it? *They all died in faith. They confessed that they were "visitors and strangers" on this earth. They were looking forward to the hope of heaven.*

How is a life different when a person lives for the hope of heaven instead of the things this world has to offer? *discuss*

10. In verses 17 through 19, we see the story of Abraham and his son Isaac. This is one of the most incredible stories of faith ever written. Read and discuss. *Verse 18 tells us that God had told Abraham that his descendents would come from Isaac, so Abraham believed that God would raise Isaac from the dead (v. 19) if need be.*

God wants us to "lay our Isaacs" on the altar. Our Isaac is anything that we love more than we love God. Sometimes God requires a sacrifice from us, and sometimes he just wants to know if we are willing to make the sacrifice. *Does anyone have an example from your own life?*

11. Verse 23 tells us that Moses' parents had faith as well. How did they act on it? *They hid him for three months.*

Verses 23 through 32 tell of Moses and others who did great things because of their faith.

Do good things always happen to faithful people? Does God always reward our faith with what we want?

At this point, I want you to read the rest of the faith chapter and discuss what is happening. Does the different treatment seem fair to us? *Good for us is our comfort and convenience, but good in God's eyes is Christian character. Romans 8:28 shares with us that when bad things happen to us, God uses them for good and makes us more like his son.*

Verses 39 and 40 tell us that sometimes God wants us to wait and share the even better rewards that were prepared for us.

Song of the week: "He's Always Been Faithful" by Sara Groves

LESSON 11

LORD, I WANT TO KNOW YOU MORE!

This is a short lesson but also a great lesson for discussion! You might talk about what each deed of the flesh means and also the meaning of each fruit.

The entire Bible shows us God's efforts to know and fellowship with us. He talked to Adam in the garden. He gave us his incredible creation to see his handiwork. He sent prophets, allowed kings, sent judges, arranged angelic visits, and finally came to earth himself. Knowing God and desiring his ways will have a profound impact on your life!

Galatians 5:16-24—the Fruit of the Spirit

1. We need to walk in the *spirit*, not in the *sinful nature*.
2. The flesh and the spirit are *contrary* to one another.
3. The deeds of the flesh are: *Sexual sin, uncleanness, lewdness (ugly language and thoughts), idolatry, sorcery, hatred, contentions, jealousies, outbursts of wrath, selfish ambitions, envy, murder, drunkenness, etc.*
4. What is the result of practicing the deeds of the flesh (v. 21)? *It hurts your relationships with others and grieves God. You will not inherit the kingdom of heaven. We all sin, but this is talking about a person who makes a regular practice of choosing a sinful lifestyle. Read Psalm 1:1-3*
5. The man who delights in the Lord will produce much what? *Fruit.*
6. Galatians 5:22-23 tells us what the fruits of the spirit are. List them. *They are love, joy, peace, longsuffering, kindness, goodness, faithfulness, gentleness, and self-control.*

What can you do to make sure you are a "fruit bearer"?
Galatians 5:25 *"Walk in the spirit."*

Spiritual breathing—Just as we exhale carbon dioxide, we spiritually exhale the sin in our lives by confessing it. Just as we breathe in oxygen, we ask God's spirit to fill and control our lives once again. (This concept was taken from Dr. Bill Bright of Campus Crusade International.)

Hang out with the right people! *Do you find yourself acting differently with different groups of friends?*

Fill up with God's goodness. Like the tree by the river, drink it in at every opportunity.

Find a version of the song, "Oh, I Want to Know You More" online and play as students listen to the words. I recommend artist Steve Green's version.

Song of the Week: "Oh, I Want to Know You More"

Encourage students to listen closely to the song, and then send them to a quiet spot to write God a letter expressing the desires of their own hearts. Also ask them to examine their lives and to "discard" any undesirable fruit.

LESSON 12

Armor of God

Prepare the craft project: Make "paper doll" cutouts, and have a picture of each student's face glued to the head portion of their doll. Cut and give each student her body and armor pieces and glue to dress the doll at the end of the lesson. Have the students write on each armor piece what that piece stands for.

"Put on the full armor of God so that you can take your stand against the devil's schemes." Ephesians 6:11

Read Ephesians 6:10-17.

1. What is armor used for, and why would Paul use this metaphor to help us "arm" ourselves as Christians? (Verse 10 gives a clue.) *It is used so that we may stand against the tricks and strategies of Satan. It is used for protection so that we might stand firm in what we believe. The only offensive weapon in God's armor is the sword of the spirit or the Word of God.*

2. What are the "wiles of the devil"? (See 2 Corinthians 11:3) *They are the lies, evil plans, and deceitfulness of Satan. This Scripture talks about the serpent deceiving Eve in the garden. He has been up to his tricks for a long time. We want to be armed so we do not fall into temptation as Eve did.*

3. In Ephesians 6:12, we learn that our battle is not with humans but with whom? *It is with Satan. It is against the rulers, authorities, and powers of this world's darkness and against the powers of evil in the spirit world.*

4. What do you make of Ephesians 6:13-14a? *As Christians we need to stand firm in our beliefs and uphold righteousness. Sometimes this is hard when everyone else is doing wrong and you know you need to be different. I Corinthians 15:33 says that "bad company corrupts good character." A good example of this is a bowl of fruit. When one piece rots, it begins spoiling the piece that it touches and so on.*

We need to be prepared *ahead of time.* Evil will come our way!

The story of the wise man who built his house upon the rock reminds me of this. It doesn't say "if" the wind and rain come; it says "when" the wind and rain come against the house. We will all have storms in our lifetimes and need to be prepared.

5. Listed below are the six pieces of armor mentioned. What does each of these represent?

- Belt—*Truth. The belt surrounds us as a reminder that the father of lies will not trip us up if we are truthful and we believe the truth of God's Word.*
- Breastplate—*Righteousness. This is to guard your heart, to help you do good, and to keep you pure.*
- Feet—*Used to spread the gospel. Be ready to go when and where God sends you.*
- Shield—*Faith. It deflects Satan's arrows. Our faith must be strong to guard our spiritual lives*
- Helmet—*Salvation. If you are wearing this, you have won the battle against death! You belong to God, and no one can snatch you away.*
- Sword—*Word of God. The Bible tells us that God's Word is "sharper than a two edged sword." We can use the Word to fight against Satan just as Jesus did when he was tempted, by quoting Scripture.*

Notice the Christian does not have anything to protect his back. We are not supposed to retreat; we are to stand firm!

Art Project: *Hand out the dolls and pieces. Let students write on each piece its meaning and glue it to the doll. Tell them to tape them to their mirror so they can memorize the parts. You might ask them which is their favorite piece of armor.*

Song of the Week: "Armor of God" by Patrick Ryan Clark

LESSON 13

Do I Have My Helmet On?

"For God so loved the world that he gave his one and only Son, that whoever believes in him shall not perish but have eternal life." John 3:16

In the last lesson we talked about putting on all of God's armor so that we could stand against the ways of Satan. This week we will talk about the crucial piece of armor that commits you to the family of God for eternity.

1. Ephesians 6:17 tells us that we are to take on the "helmet of *salvation*." What do you think this could mean? *Let the students give their answers, and then tell them, "Let's look and see what the word salvation means and what God's Word says about it."*
2. Look up the word "salvation" in the dictionary and record the meaning here. *It means deliverance from destruction*
3. What do we, as humans, need to be saved from? Romans 3:23 *Sin. We have all sinned and fall short of the glory of God. Genesis 4:7 says, "If you do what is right, will you not be accepted? But if you do not do what is right, sin is crouching at your door; it desires to have you, but you must master it."*

God created us for his pleasure, to walk with him in the garden and to be companions for him. We, like Adam and Eve, from time to time, follow our own sinful desires and break off companionship with him. He is a holy God and can have no fellowship with our rebellious life of sin.

4. Romans 6:23 tells us, "The wages of sin is *death*."

Remember the different sacrifices that Cain and Abel offered to God for their sins? Remember the strict laws of the Old Testament and the animal sacrifices? Remember the priests and judges whose jobs were to point out and help people deal with their sins?
In the New Testament God reveals the provision he has made for us to deal with our sin problem *directly*. It is through the sacrifice and the shedding of his son's blood.

43

5. Romans 5:8 *"God demonstrates his own love for us in this: While we were still sinners, Christ died for us."*

   John 14:6 *"Jesus answered, I am the way, and the truth, and the life. No one comes to the Father except through me."*

   Romans 8:1a *"Therefore, there is now no condemnation for those who are in Christ Jesus."* In other words, we are sinful and cannot approach God. He has made a way for us to have fellowship with him by offering his son. Why he chose to do it this way is a mystery to us, but he is God. His ways are not our ways; they are higher and better. There is something that we must do individually with his wonderful provision!

6. John 1:12 says, "Yet to all who *received* him, to those who *believed* in his name, he gave the right to become children of God."

*Is this **all** that God **requires** of us? (Surely we must be missionaries, sing in the choir, give to the poor, and never cuss or fuss!)*

7. Ephesians 2:8-9 says "For it *is by grace* you have been *saved*, through *faith*—and this not from *yourselves*, it is the *gift* of God—not by *works*, so that no one can boast."

He desires a relationship with *you!* It is a *free* gift, *you don't* have to work for it—only believe and receive it. Honestly, is there *anything* that we could do that would ever merit this wonderful gift?

8. In Revelation 3:20, Christ says, "Here I am! I stand at the door and knock. If anyone hears my voice and opens the door, I will come in and eat with him, and he with me."

If you have never invited Christ into your life, this would be a good time. His desire is that none should perish but all experience *his abundant* life and have everlasting life with him. You may do so by praying and asking forgiveness for your sins and by telling God you appreciate him sending his son to make a provision for the forgiveness of your sins. By doing so, you are telling God that you would like him to take and control your life and produce the kind of fruit in you that comes from knowing and following him.

Prayer Opportunity: You may lead students aloud or let them pray silently. A sample prayer might be: Lord Jesus, thank you for dying on the cross to take away my sins. I know that I am a sinner and want your forgiveness. You tell me if I will ask, you will come into my heart, and I want to do that now. Thank you that you promise to never leave me.

9. Did you ask God into your life? According to Revelation 3:20, where is he? *He is in your heart.*
10. What wonderful promise do we find in Hebrew 13:5? *He will never leave you!*

Congratulations if you prayed this prayer today *for the first time!* You are a new baby in the family of God. It is great that you are in a Bible study so you can *grow* and learn from his Word.

For those of you who have already accepted Christ as your Savior, I pray that you are *growing* in your walk with God. What advice would you give a new Christian?

Let the students share their own experience in becoming a Christian. This can be very powerful for new believers to hear from their peers.

What if you *sometimes* have doubts that you might not be a Christian sometime? Where do you think that kind of thinking comes from? What does the Bible (the eternal Word of God) tell you? Hebrews 13:5 says *He will never leave you!*

Song of the week: "Give Me Your Eyes" by Brandon Heath

LESSON 14

Empty Me So I Can Be Filled with You

Once you have made a decision to "believe and receive" what should you do next?

Paul is writing to the new church in Philippi. Philippians 2:3-15 says: (Have students fill in the blanks):

Do nothing out of _selfish ambition_ or _vain conceit_, but in _humility_ consider others better than yourselves. Each of you should look not only to your own interests, but also to the interests of _others_. Your attitude should be the same as that of Christ Jesus: Who, being in very nature God, did not consider _equality_ with God something to be grasped, but made himself _nothing_, taking the very nature of a _servant_, being made in human likeness. And being found in appearance as a _man_, he humbled himself and became _obedient_ to death—even death on a cross! Therefore God exalted him to the highest place and gave him the name that is above every name, that at the name of Jesus every _knee should bow_, in heaven and on earth and under the earth, and every tongue confess that Jesus Christ is Lord, to the glory of God the Father. Therefore, my dear friends, as you have always _obeyed_—not only in my presence, but now much more in my absence—continue to work out your salvation with fear and trembling, for it is God who works in you to will and to act according to his good _purpose_. Do everything without _complaining_ and _arguing_, so that you may become _blameless_ and _pure_, children of God without fault in a _crooked_ and _depraved_ generation, in which you shine like _stars_ in the universe.

The words "made himself nothing" are translated "made himself empty." Just as Christ emptied himself on the cross, so must we empty ourselves of sin, selfishness, pride, arrogance, and seeking our will before his. God didn't have to become a man. The man Christ didn't have to become a servant. The servant man did not have to die for us. The death didn't have to be a cruel one on a cross.

_He_ is _our_ example of a Christian life. God allowed Christ to become a man to _identify_ with us!

1. What was Christ's attitude toward others while he hung on the cross?
   - John 19:26-27 (concerning his mother) *He asked John to take care of her.*
   - Luke 23:34 (concerning those crucifying him) *He showed forgiveness.*
   - Luke 23:40-43 (concerning the criminal being crucified with him) *He showed him compassion and hope.*
2. How can you empty yourself of *you* to make room for *God's* agenda? It must be a conscious effort! *Suggestions of answer: Confess sin in your life, ask the Holy Spirit to take control, read his Word, make your walk match your talk, attend church, pray, attend Bible study.*
3. From the Philippians Scripture, list as many things as you can find from which you desire to be emptied. *Some examples are selfish ambition, vain conceit, complaining and arguing, etc.*
4. What was Christ's attitude, and how could it help you to follow his example? *His attitude was one of humility and considering others better than himself. He had the attitude of a servant and was blameless and pure.*
5. Who can you think of that could benefit from your obedience to Christ? *Everyone can benefit, friends and family alike!*
6. How can you shine like a star in a crooked and depraved world? *Display your fruits (love, joy, peace, patience, kindness, goodness, faithfulness, gentleness and self-control).*

Anyway
Author Unknown

People are unreasonable, illogical and self-centered. Love them *anyway.*
If you do good, people will accuse you of selfish motives. Do good *anyway.*
The kindness you show today may be forgotten tomorrow. Be kind *anyway.*
What you spend years building may be destroyed overnight. Build *anyway.*
People really need help but may attack you if you help them. Help them *anyway.*
Give the world the best you've got and you might get kicked in the teeth. Give the best you've got *anyway.*

Don't you want to empty yourself to make room for what God can do in your life? Don't you want to *shine* for him?

Song of the week: "Empty Me" by Chris Sligh

LESSON 15

Taming the Tongue

"Do not merely listen to the word, and so deceive yourselves. Do what it says."
James 1:22

One of the words you hear a lot of teenagers use today is *drama*. Drama can be used to describe actions, of course, but it can start and also manifest itself in speech. Let's face it, girls like to talk, and sometimes that talk can lead to *gossip*. What would you consider to be "gossip"? *It could be sharing something someone has asked you not to or spreading something that you don't know to be true.*

There is an old saying, "Sticks and stones can break my bones but words will never hurt me." Do you think this is true? How does it make you feel when someone has spread something about you that is not true? Can it ruin your friendship?

Let's look at just how much power the tongue has!

Read James 3:3-4. What two things does James compare the tongue to? *He compares it to a bit and a rudder. Discuss the fact that they are very small parts but have a great influence on the guidance of a horse and ship.*

These two small items have a huge impact on their subject. Get the picture! Read James 3:5-6. These verses even take things a step further. What power does the tongue have in this illustration? *It has the power of total ruin and devastation. A big forest fire can be started with only a little flame.*

Remember what Smokey the Bear says: "Only *you* can prevent *forest fires*."

Have you ever had that "uh oh" feeling right before you said something that you shouldn't? I believe it is the Holy Spirit's guidance, a clear warning that you should just clam up! After you clam up, think: (Psalm 19:14) *"May the words of my mouth and the meditation of my heart be pleasing in your sight, Oh Lord, my Rock and my redeemer"*

Remember, one of our fruits of the spirit is self-control. What do I Peter 3:10, Proverbs 15:28, and Proverbs 16:23 suggest?

- I Peter 3:10: *Keep your tongue from evil and your lips from deceitful speech.*
- Proverbs 15:28: *"The heart of the righteous weighs its answers, but the mouth of the wicked gushes evil."*
- Proverbs 16:23: *"A wise man's heart guides his mouth, and his lips promote instruction."*

Even better, let's use our speech for building our friends up! What does a trustworthy friend do? Proverbs 11:13 *"A gossip betrays a confidence, but a trustworthy man keeps a secret."* A good friend conceals the matter and keeps the secret.

I'm sure you've all had the experience when someone said a kind word at just the right time. It can mean the world to you. You might have just been sitting in the cafeteria alone and a friend invited you to join her at the table. It's great to feel accepted. The Bible says that a word spoken in the right circumstances is like: (Proverbs 25:11) *"apples of gold in settings of silver" Discuss this word picture.*

Edwin Markham (1852-1940) wrote a little poem that went like this:

> He drew a circle that shut me out—
> Heretic, rebel, a thing to flout.
> But love and I had the wit to win,
> We drew a circle that took him in!

Read Proverbs 17:17. It tells us that a true friend loves when? *At all times!* We all mess up from time to time. If you don't listen to the "uh oh" call of the spirit and go ahead and share something about a friend that you shouldn't, what should you do to make things right with that person and with God? *You should ask forgiveness.*

If you were children, I would remind you of the song, "Oh be careful little mouth what you say." Our little mouths can have big consequences.

Thought: While chatting with your fingers when you are texting, on Twitter, e-mailing, and on Facebook, think long and hard before you hit the send button. Don't send something that you wouldn't want anybody else to read or that you will regret later!

Song of the week: "Do Everything" by Steven Curtis Chapman

LESSON 16

Pretty Is as Pretty Does

"Like a gold ring in a pig's snout is a beautiful woman who shows no discretion."
Proverbs 11:22

Describe a "lady" in your own words. *She would contain the fruit of the spirit. Her appearance and speech should reflect Godliness.*

Describe a "woman worthy of praise" in your own words. *She is a hard worker and looks after the needs of others.*

Can you think of any "worthy ladies" who would be good role models for young girls today?

Proverbs 31:30 says, "Charm is deceptive, and beauty is fleeting; but a woman who fears the Lord is to be praised." Discuss the meaning of this verse.
Inward beauty is more important than outward beauty.

Proverbs 31:31 says, "Give her the reward she has earned, and let her works bring her praise at the city gate." Discuss the meaning of this verse. *She has a reputation for doing good. Talk about the importance of a good reputation.*

You might say "her reputation precedes her." Have you ever heard the saying, "Reputations are like fine china, easily broken and hard to repair"?

What actions can bring a girl a good reputation (remember our fruits of the spirit)? *Discuss.* What actions do you think bring a girl a bad reputation? *Discuss.*

Let's look back at Galatians 5:19-21. What actions does the Bible tell us to avoid?

It tells us to avoid following our own inclinations. This produces evil results, impure thoughts, eagerness for lustful pleasure, idolatry, spiritism, hatred and fighting, jealousy and anger, constant effort to get the best for yourself, complaints and criticisms, the feeling that everyone else is wrong except those in your own little group, wrong doctrine, envy, murder, drunkenness, wild parties, and all that sort of thing.

What can you do to avoid these behaviors and their effects on your life? *Stay grounded in God's Word. Choose your friends wisely. Follow God's commands.*

An old expression says, "If you lie down with dogs you will get up with fleas." Proverbs 13:20 states it differently. Write out this verse and discuss. *"He who walks with the wise grows wise, but a companion of fools suffers harm."*

Can you see how the friends you run with can greatly influence you?

While we like to blame our sinful actions on the influence of others, we alone are responsible for our actions. The world offers more impure opportunities than ever before, but the same temptations that are pulling on you have been around ever since the Garden of Eden. It is up to you to decide, "Am I going to follow the ways of the Lord or the deeds of the flesh?"

How can you ever begin to escape all the temptations that are surrounding you? The escape begins in your *mind*. Philippians 4:8 tells us to think about what? *Things that are true and good and right and pure and lovely. We should dwell on the fine and good things in others. We should think about the things for which we can praise God.*

Is this the way you naturally think? Of course not! You must decide that your desire is to follow God and that you want to please him. Romans 12:2 says that you must be "transformed by the renewing of your mind."

Below are four different areas in which teens will have to face decisions on how God would have them behave. Remember, pretty is as pretty does.

1) **Your Body and Appearance**

   I Corinthians 6:19-20 *"Do you not know that your body is a temple of the Holy Spirit, who is in you, whom you have received from God? You are not your own; you were bought at a price. Therefore honor God with your body."*

   All of these things fall into this category: skin care, weight, oral hygiene, sleep, drugs, smoking, posture and sitting, and "lazy language."
   What about your appearance? I Timothy 2:9-10 *"I also want women to dress modestly, with decency and propriety, not with braided hair or gold or pearls or expensive clothes,"*
   Have you ever watched the TV show *What Not to Wear*? What does the way you dress say about you?

2) How You Spend Your Time

Are you preparing yourself for greatness or just biding your time? Do you study properly? Do you waste time in front of the TV? Are you thinking constantly about what would please you or are you considering the needs of others?

3) How Do You Treat Your Parents?

One of the Ten Commandments is Exodus 20:12 which states: "Honor your father and your mother, so that you may live long in the land the Lord your God is giving you."

Ephesians 6:1 "Children obey your parents in the Lord, for this is right."
Proverbs 4:20-23 "Your parents' advice will keep you from harm."

4) Dating (Next Lesson)

Song of the week: "My Heart Your Home" by Christy Nockels

LESSON 17

Dating

"Don't let anyone look down on you because you are young, but set an example for the believers in speech, in life, in love, in faith and in purity." I Timothy 4:12

I chose a positive verse for this lesson because I think dating should be a positive and fun experience. Being noticed by boys and interacting with them is fun and exciting! Tell me what the dating world is like today. Do you have an age limit for when you can single date? What are your some of your parents' rules about dating? *Discuss.*

It is interesting to read stories of romantic encounters in the Bible. I can just picture Naomi getting Ruth all "gussied" up to go and meet Boaz and Esther putting on her royal robes and jewels to meet with King Ahasuerus and trying to persuade him to save her people. God has given you beauty and charms to attract the opposite sex. After all, God made boys so darn cute that we couldn't help but be attracted to them. Thank goodness he has also given us guidelines in his Word for a healthy dating experience. As a Christian, your dating life should be quite different from the swept away, instant romance, sexual episodes you see portrayed in movies, TV, and romance novels.

What insight does the Bible give us in this area? The Scriptures don't say a lot about the actual dating process, but they do assure you that God has a specific plan for your life (Jer. 29:11), and that we are to be careful about who we choose to date (II Cor. 6:14). There are also many Scriptures that warn us to stay sexually pure (II Tim. 2:22, 1 Cor. 6:18, 1 Thess. 4:3-5, Eph. 5:3).

1) How does the media today portray dating, romance and sex to the average teen?
   Magazines have sexual headlines and cover stories. Books have suggestive titles and covers. TV and movies are pretty much "anything goes." Seldom do you see young people restricting sexual activity at all. Sex is portrayed as "noncommittal," which could not be further from the truth.

As you can see, God's ideals are far different from the world's view, and the consequences from ignoring God can be heartbreaking. There is no other area in life that causes as many regrets as being sexually impure.

2) What are some of the regrets you might experience as a result of diving in too fast and too far with the opposite sex? *You set yourself up for emotional heartbreak! You could destroy your parents' trust and your relationship with them and break their hearts. You could become pregnant, and that opens up a whole different set of problems. You could get AIDS or other sexually transmitted diseases.*

3) What happens to us when we don't heed God's advice in any area of our lives? Proverbs 1:29-31 says, *"Since they hated knowledge and did not choose to fear the Lord, since they would not accept my advice and spurned my rebuke, they will eat the fruit of their ways and be filled with the fruit of their schemes."*

What are some ways you can "trouble proof" your dating life and get the most enjoyment from it? *Discuss.*

Purity is one of your most precious possessions.

Look up the word "pure" in the dictionary. *It means unmixed with any other matter, free from dirt or taint, spotless, stainless, free from moral fault or guilt. (Merriam-Webster's Collegiate Dictionary. 10th Edition. 1996).*

Once again, where does impurity begin? *It begins in your mind.* You must *guard* what you see, listen to, and allow your mind to think about.

The Internet and Pornography

Pornography is so easy to access with the Internet. Once you view something, it has passed the gate—your eyes—into your mind. Then it is there forever. The image is never to be erased. Satan would just love to fill your mind with filth.

Ted Bundy, a serial killer in the 1970s and 1980s, said his cruel murders of some thirty women and young girls all began with his desire to look at pornography. *Look online for a short video clip of part of James Dobson's death row interview with Ted Bundy and show students.*

The popular television show *Dateline* shows sting operations of perverts preying on young women via the Internet. *This is nothing to play with!* Stay away from unwholesome websites.

I blame part of the problem of sexual permissiveness on my generation. We have been far too "tolerant" and have not sought and taught God's Word as instructed. Titus 2:3-5

"Likewise, teach the older women to be reverent in the way they live, not to be slanderers or addicted to much wine, but to teach what is good. Then they can train the younger women to love their husbands and children, to be self-controlled and pure, to be busy at home, to be kind, and to be subject to their husbands, so that no one will malign the word of God."

Pearls of Wisdom from Proverbs

Proverbs 4:11-12: *"I guide you in the way of wisdom and lead you along straight paths. When you walk, your steps will not be hampered; when you run, you will not stumble."*

Proverbs 4:23: *"Above all else, guard your heart, for it is the wellspring of life."*

Proverbs 15:14: *"The discerning heart seeks knowledge, but the mouth of a fool feeds on folly."* (There is plenty of it out there to feed on, as we discussed earlier!)

Proverbs 19:23: *"The fear of the Lord leads to life: Then one rests content, untouched by trouble."*

Song of the week: "He Leadeth Me" by Candi Pearson

LESSON 18

ANY VESSEL CAN BE USED—THE STORY OF RAHAB

Read Joshua chapters 2 and 6. The main characters of this story are Joshua, Rahab, and the two spies.

1) Joshua was leading the Israelites into the promised land of *Canaan.*
2) He sent *two spies* into the city of *Jericho*, one of the most wicked cities.
3) Rahab was a *prostitute* and lived on the outer wall to the city, a prime location for her occupation.
4) How do you think Rahab and the people of Jericho had heard of the Israelites before they reached Jericho? *Joshua 2:10 says, "We have heard how the Lord dried up the water of the Red Sea for you when you came out of Egypt, and what you did to Sihon and Og, the two kings of the Amorites east of the Jordan, whom you completely destroyed."*
5) Even in those early days, news of this magnitude would travel from city to city! What miraculous events are we told of in the journey of escape from Egypt? *We are told about the parting of the Red Sea, the pillar of fire, manna from heaven, the Ten Commandments, the burning bush, etc.*

Rahab had heard the stories of how God had helped the Israelites escape slavery and the miracles he had performed in the desert. Their story had **inspired** her and she chose to believe in God as well. When the spies entered her home she knew she could be killed for hiding them but chose rather to act on her new faith. She believed that God could spare her and her family if they were overtaken in an attack by the Israelites.

6) Joshua and the Israelites destroyed the city. What became of Rahab and her family? *They were spared as promised.*

At some moment in your life, you heard of God and his *love for you. You had to make a decision* to accept or to reject him. Your belief in God, just like Rahab's, can change your destiny. He can take any life, no matter what the situation, and turn it around. One great biblical example is Paul, a man who once hated and persecuted Christians. He later became a mighty man of God and authored much of the New Testament.

Matthew 1:5 *"Salmon was the father of Boaz, whose mother was Rahab."* This is the genealogy list of Jesus Christ.

Hebrews 11:31 *"By faith the prostitute Rahab, because she welcomed the spies, was not killed with those who were disobedient."* Rahab is listed in Hebrews 11, the roll call of the faithful!

James 2:25 *"In the same way, was not even Rahab the prostitute considered righteous for what she did when she gave lodging to the spies and sent them off in a different direction?"*

Rahab received an extraordinary inheritance for her faith. How was she honored? *She was in the blood line of Jesus. She was the mother of Boaz and in the ancestry of King David. Not only did she show her faith, but she also bravely acted upon it*

It doesn't matter what your limitations are or what your past is. It is not what the vessel is made of that matters; it is what fills it! If given the opportunity, God can direct a heart and use any of us, just like he did Rehab.

Matthew 10:8 reminds us that freely we have received and freely we should give.
There is no doubt that you can use this story many times in your life. When you have a friend who has sinned and feels like there is no hope, what a wonderful example Rahab could be.

Salvation, conversion, or trusting God can be broken down into three categories: 1) life before knowing God, 2) time of believing, 3) life after surrendering to God. These three categories make up your Christian testimony.

Song of the week: "Basics of Life" by 4 Him

LESSON 19

PRAYER

Prepare: Have a bar of soap for every student with the verse 1 John 1:9 glued to it. Hand them out when you answer question 3.

"Let us then approach the throne of grace with confidence, so that we may receive mercy and find grace to help us in our time of need." Hebrews 4:16

When we pray, we connect to the awesome God who created this amazing universe. We can come to him at any time, day or night. He will not be asleep. His line will not be busy. We will not hear, "All of our operators are assisting other customers." What an incredible privilege we have to fellowship with an ever-available, loving heavenly Father and lay all our concerns before him.

Does it seem to you that some people have a closer connection with heaven than others? Do some people seem to have more prayers answered? Are there certain people you would want praying for you because you are sure they have a more direct hotline?

1) Can some people really pray more effectively than others? James 5:16b *"The prayer of a righteous man is powerful and effective."*

The Bible tells us that all have sinned, and that no one is righteous. So how can we become righteous and have a more effective prayer life? II Corinthians 5:21 tells us that through Christ we can become right with God. He made this possible at the cross. We could say that the first condition for an effective prayer life is to belong to God by accepting Christ and having our sins forgiven.

2) Are all Christians able to pray effectively?

Psalm 66:18 *"If I had cherished sin in my heart, the Lord would not have listened;"*
Isaiah 59:2 *"But your iniquities have separated you from your God; your sins have hidden his face from you, so that he will not hear."*

3) God has made a provision for the Christian who has sinned. I John 1:9 has been called "the Christian's bar of soap." Write it here: *"If we confess our sins, he is faithful and just and will forgive us our sins and purify us from all unrighteousness."*

So if we want to pray effectively, we need to first confess our sins and allow God to cleanse us. When we ask God to reveal our sins and then confess them, he will cleanse us from all unrighteousness, even those things we may have forgotten or may not have recognized as sin. Not only does God forgive our sins, but he also forgets them. If we come to him and say, "Oh Lord, I've done it again," he will say, "Done what?"

We have seen two conditions for praying effectively: accepting Christ and keeping our sins confessed. There are also some other conditions that will enable us to pray even more effectively.

4) Read John 15:7 *"If you remain in me and my words remain in you, ask whatever you wish, and it will be given you."*

5) What does it mean to "remain in Christ?" *It means to abide, stay, or walk closely.*

6) What does it mean for God's word to "remain in us?" *It means we feed on it, learn it, memorize it, and live it.*

Most of us know more of God's principles than we are doing.

7) I John 3:22 underscores obedience and gives us another condition. What is it? *It says, "and receive from him anything we ask, because we obey his commands and do what pleases him."*

8) What could be the difference between keeping God's commandments and doing those things that are pleasing to him? *We keep his commands out of obedience to him, but we do so lovingly and faithfully to please him. An example might be when your mother asks you to clean your room. There is a difference in "just getting the job done" to be obedient and doing the job extra nice to please her.*

Another condition is faith! Mark 11:24 *"Therefore I tell you, whatever you ask for in prayer, believe that you have received it, and it will be yours."*

9) How can we increase our faith? Romans 10:17 *"Consequently, faith comes from hearing the message, and the message is heard through the word of Christ."*

As we trust God in situation after situation, we experience his faithfulness and come to rely on it every time. Our faith also grows as we share our lives with other Christians and are encouraged by seeing and hearing how God is working in their lives. *This is one of the benefits of Bible study!*

10) What is another condition of prayer that is found in James 4:3? *"When you ask, you do not receive, because you ask with wrong motives, that you may spend what you get on your pleasures." God's plan should come first. He alone knows what is best for us.*

This may give insight as to why some of our prayers have not been answered. God may give us an answer to our prayers other than yes. He may say no, maybe, or wait and see. He may give us something much better than what we have requested. Someone has said, "God gives the best to those who leave the choice with him." If God isn't always going to give us what we ask for, why should we pray? James tells us, "We have not because we ask not." God is willing to give us many things if we but ask.

11) Is asking God for what we want the only reason to pray? What other reasons are there? *No, we can give him praise, seek his will, intercede for others, thank him, ask for guidance, etc.*

What an honor and privilege to be able to praise him, thank him, enjoy fellowship with him, and just "be still" and listen to what he has to say to you!

Song of the week: "Be Still and Know" by Steven Curtis Chapman

LESSON 20

FORGIVENESS

"Be kind and compassionate to one another, forgiving each other, just as in Christ God forgave you." Ephesians 4:32

Unfortunately, people in our lives will sometimes say or do things that hurt us. How do you find yourself reacting when this happens to you? *Discuss.*

What makes people be unkind to other people? It is really more about them and who they are trying to be than it is about you. *Discuss.*

Does the Bible have things to say about forgiving those who have mistreated us? Is this an easy or hard thing to do? *Discuss.*

Why Should We Forgive?

There are several reasons. The main reason is that Jesus told us to forgive, and that's reason enough by itself.

1) Read Matthew 18:21-22: *"Then Peter came to Jesus and asked, "Lord, how many times shall I forgive my brother when he sins against me? Up to seven times?" Jesus answered, "I tell you, not seven times, but seventy-seven times."* Do you think Jesus meant for us to count the times we've forgiven someone else and withhold forgiveness after so many times? *No.*

We should forgive others so God will forgive us. We pray in the Lord's Prayer, "Father, forgive us as we forgive those that trespass against us."

2) What do Matthew 6:14-15 and Luke 6:37 have to say on this subject? *Matthew 6:14-15 says "For if you forgive men when they sin against you, your heavenly Father will also forgive you. But if you do not forgive men their sins, your Father*

will not forgive your sins." Luke 6:37 says, "Do not judge, and you will not be judged. Do not condemn, and you will not be condemned. Forgive, and you will be forgiven."

We should forgive others so God will hear our prayers. Since God has told us to forgive offenses against us, unforgiveness is a sin.

3)   These two verses tell us what about our sin of unforgiveness?

Psalm 66:18 *"If I had cherished sin in my heart, the Lord would not have listened;"* Isaiah 59:2 *"But your iniquities have separated you from your God; your sins have hidden his face from you, so that he will not hear."*

When we have sin in our lives, God does not listen to us.

It has been said that acid can corrode the vessel that contains it. The person who is hurt most by an unforgiving attitude is not the one who has done wrong but the one who refuses to forgive. The person who has hurt us doesn't even realize we are thinking mean thoughts, but those thoughts steal our enjoyment of life. We can be at a fun party or a sleepover at our best friend's house, but the bitterness in our hearts takes away the pleasure we should have.

4)   Hebrews 12:15 could help in this situation. Write it here :*It says, "See to it that no one misses the grace of God and that no bitter root grows up to cause trouble and defile many." How do you have to get rid of weeds? They must be uprooted or they will come back!*

You may say, "I can forgive, but I can't forget." The memory of abuse from others does linger in our memory banks, but we have a choice. We can go over and over the details in our minds and feel the hurt all over again, or when we are tempted to do that, we can focus elsewhere, especially on God's grace and goodness to us. What is the hardest thing you have had to forgive?

I marvel at those who have *forgiven* the brutal, senseless murders of one of their loved ones. One example is the family of Rachel Scott, a teenager who was killed in the Columbine High School shooting. Here is their story entitled, "What Role Does Forgiveness Play in Overcoming Tragedy?" by Beth Nimmo and Darrell Scott (found in the *The Answer Bible*):

> People respond differently to tragedy when it strikes their lives. Some never get over it. Others become bitter and angry, and that is easily understandable. However, we are given the opportunity to experience a realm of grace that is incomprehensible to some when we choose to forgive. Were we angry when our daughter Rachel Scott was killed in the shootings at Columbine High School? Yes! Were we sad? Beyond description! But are we forgiving? That

is probably one of the most difficult issues to face when you have been so deeply wronged.

Our understanding of God's heart left us only one choice, the decision to forgive. It was the choice of Jesus as He hung on a cross dying. He said in Matthew 5:43-44: "You have heard that it was said, 'Love your neighbor and hate your enemy.' But I tell you: Love your enemies and pray for those who persecute you."

Forgiveness is not just for the offender. It is also for the one who is offended. If we do not forgive, we end up in perpetual anger and bitterness and eventually offend others with our words or actions. If we forgive, we experience a "letting go" or cleansing process that frees us from the offender.

There is a great misunderstanding about forgiveness. Forgiveness is not pardon. Forgiveness is an attitude, while pardon is an action. Had they lived, we would not have pardoned these boys for what they did. In fact, I (Darrell) would have killed them to prevent the slaughter that occurred if I had been given the chance. I believe most people would have done the same. If they had lived, we would have testified against them and demanded that justice be done. However, our hearts toward them could not have harbored unforgiveness. Unforgiveness blocks God's ability to flow through us to help others.

God wants us to overcome evil with good. Such a thing is beyond human ability, but it is possible when we acknowledge our weakness and submit to God's grace. *The Answer Bible* taken from *Rachel's Tears by Beth Nimmo and Darrell Scott* (Word Publishing, A Division of Thomas Nelson, 2003) p 1153.

Forgiveness is required of us if we are to live healthy, non-bitter, God-pleasing lives.

Song of the week: "Amazing Love" by Christine Young

LESSON 21

CONFIDENT LIVING

"For God did not give us a spirit of timidity, but a spirit of power, of love and of self-discipline." II Timothy 1:7

(My inspiration came from a sermon by my beloved pastor, Terry Greer, and I have used some of his illustrations.)

1) Read Romans 8:12-15. We as Christians are *adopted* by God! Does this give you comfort?

2) What is fear? *Use the dictionary! One dictionary definition is, "An unpleasant often strong emotion caused by anticipation or awareness of danger."(Merriam-Webster's Collegiate Dictionary. 10th Edition. 1996).*

3) What are most people afraid of? Come up with a top ten list of your own. *I have given suggestions:*

    1. *Spiders*
    2. *Heights*
    3. *Public speaking*
    4. *Crowds*
    5. *Thunder*
    6. *Cancer*
    7. *Flying*
    8. *Needles*
    9. *Confined spaces*
    10. *Death*

People can be weighed down or even paralyzed by fear! It can drain your energy and take away your power. You can become unhappy and nonproductive.

4. Write out II Timothy 1:7: *"For God did not give us a spirit of timidity, but a spirit of power, of love and of self-discipline."*

5) How can you avoid fear and enjoy God's power? John 15:7 says, *"If you remain in me and my words remain in you, ask whatever you wish, and it will be given you." Remain in God.* How do you remain in Him? Use what God gave you! Use your eyes to read his word and take it into your mind, to be applied to your heart. Use your ears to listen to sermons, teaching, and music that would glorify God and edify you.

As a teenage girl, I became curious about demon possession. The more I read about this subject (and I did use Christian resources), the more I opened my mind to the dealings of Satan, and the more afraid I became. One night my father came in my room and could sense my anxiousness and fear. He proceeded to throw away all the books and literature I had read. Then he prayed with me. He gave me some good advice that night when he told me to stop thinking about Satan and to concentrate on the things of Christ. I was not focusing on a healthy subject; this is one reason I discourage horror movies and some video games.

Power, Love and a Sound Mind!

Power

Ask God, relying on his infinite wisdom, to help you. You are speaking to the creator of the universe. Is any situation too large or small for him? The only power that can counteract fear is the power of faith. Pray before you face a fearful situation or when you are in one. Know that he can give you a "peace that passes all understanding." Also realize that you learn and grow spiritually by going through hard situations. Satan can be more powerful than we are, but God is more powerful than Satan.

I John 4:4 *"You, dear children, are from God and have overcome them, because the one who is in you is greater than the one who is in the world."*

James 4:7 *"Submit yourselves, then to God. Resist the devil, and he will flee from you."*

Love

There are different types of *love.* I believe this verse is referring to two kinds of love. The first is *storge* love, which gives needed support and care. This kind of love is shown in good times and bad. The other kind of love is *agape* love, an unconditional love that endures selflessly.

Sound Mind

What does it mean to have a *sound mind?* You don't depend upon emotions but rather use grounded, straight, logical thinking without prejudice. Think according to the facts.

Sometimes you do not think this way because you are upset. What might you do in this situation? *Seek the opinion of someone who has your best interest in mind.*

6) How can an "unsound" mind develop? *Discuss. It could stem from being fearful, selfish thinking, lack of knowledge, not knowing the facts, not knowing Scripture, or not listening to God or acting on advice God has given you.*

Sometimes we tend to make "knee jerk" reactions without thinking things through! As Christians, we are to seek God's counsel first. We are to know Scripture so we can apply God's thoughts to our situations. When we react to fearful situations under our own power, sin usually results. Instead of responding with love, we tend to lash out or hold in feelings of hatred and bitterness.

Hebrews 12:15 instructs us to "pluck" bitterness out by the roots, never allowing it to grow. If we do not, our sins will fester and infect every aspect of our lives. They are a foreign substance to our bodies if we are believers.

How Do I Deal with This Kind of Fear?

1. *Seek outside help.*
2. *Get the straight facts.*
3. *Get out of the situation causing fear.*
4. *Ask God to take away your fear, and trust him to do it.*
5. *Ask forgiveness if needed.*

There are 366 "Fear nots" in the Bible.

Is God showing you anything in your life from which you need to be freed?

Song of the week: "Fear Not" by Justin Davis

LESSON 22

Heaven

"For to me, to live is Christ and to die is gain. If I am to go on living in the body, this will mean fruitful labor for me. Yet what shall I choose? I do not know! I am torn between the two: I desire to depart and be with Christ, which is better by far;" Philippians 1:21-23

What if tonight, after supper, your parents called you and your brothers and sisters together and announced that your family would be moving to a new city, a place you had never been before? What questions might you ask? Discuss. (Where is it? What is it like? What recreation facilities do they have? What is the school like?) How might you find out what the new city is like? Discuss. (Visit, talk to people who live there, look on the Internet.)

Shouldn't we even be more interested in the place where we hope to spend eternity? How long is eternity? Forever!

1) Where do we get our ideas about what heaven is like? *They come from accounts of near-death experiences, movies, music, etc.*
2) Are near-death experiences for real? *I can't say for sure one way or another. They are experiences. As Christians, our source of certain knowledge is the Bible.* The Bible has over 582 references to heaven in some 550 verses.
3) Is heaven a real place? John 14:2-3 *"In my Father's house are many rooms; if it were not so, I would have told you. I am going there to prepare a place for you. And if I go and prepare a place for you, I will come back and take you to be with me that you also may be where I am." Yes, it is a real place. It is where God lives. It is his home.*
4) What does heaven look like? The apostle John was given a wonderful vision of heaven while he was in exile on an island called Patmos, and this is the fullest description we have of heaven in the Bible.

Revelation 4:3 *"And the one who sat there had the appearance of jasper and carnelian. A rainbow, resembling an emerald, encircles the throne." The throne with God on it is the centerpiece of heaven. The rainbows we see are arcs—incomplete—but the rainbow around the throne is a circle—complete. There is much light, and many precious stones are mentioned in the descriptions of heaven.*

Revelation 4:4 *"Surrounding the throne were twenty-four other thrones, and seated on them were twenty-four elders. They were dressed in white and had crowns of gold on their heads." We don't know who they are. They may be the heads of the twelve tribes of Israel in the Old Testament and the twelve apostles in the New Testament.*

Revelation 4:6 *"Also before the throne there was what looked like a sea of glass, clear as crystal."*

Revelation 21:11-14, 19, 21 *"It shone with the glory of God, and its brilliance was like that of a very precious jewel, like a jasper, clear as crystal. It had a great, high wall with twelve gates, and with twelve angels at the gates. On the gates were written the names of the twelve tribes of Israel. There were three gates on the east, three on the north, three on the south and three on the west. The wall of the city had twelve foundations, and on them were the names of the twelve apostles of the Lamb . . . The foundations of the city walls were decorated with every kind of precious stone . . . The twelve gates were twelve pearls, each gate made of a single pearl. The great street of the city was of pure gold, like transparent glass." There really are pearly gates and streets of gold.*

Heaven is a place of *"no mores."*

Revelation 21:3-4, *"And I heard a loud voice from the throne saying, "Now the dwelling of God is with men, and he will live with them. They will be his people, and God himself will be with them and be their God. He will wipe every tear from their eyes. There will be no more death or mourning or crying or pain, for the old order of things has passed away."*
Think about it . . .

    A. No more sorrow, and no more tears.
    B. No more sickness—doctors, hospitals, medicine, pain.
    C. No more death—cemeteries, funerals.
    D. No more crime—murder, jails, police. Revelation 21:27 *"Nothing impure will ever enter it, nor will anyone who does what is shameful and deceitful, but only those whose names are written in the Lamb's Book of Life."*

John was separated from those he loved by the sea that surrounded the island of Patmos. In heaven we will be reunited with our loved ones, never to experience the pain and loneliness of being separated from them again. Is there someone you are looking forward very much to seeing in heaven?

5) Will we be angels in heaven, have wings, and play harps? *No, angels are a different order of created beings.*

Psalm 8:4-5a says, *"What is man that you are mindful of him, the son of man that you care for him? You made him a little lower than the heavenly beings and crowned him with glory and honor."*

Hebrews 1:14 says, *"Are not all angels ministering spirits sent to serve those who will inherit salvation?"*

6) Will we be ourselves in heaven? I think yes! There is a principle of continuity in Scripture and in nature. If we sow a wheat seed, it produces wheat. If we sow corn, corn grows. Each plant and animal reproduces after its own kind, so I think there will be continuity in ourselves and our personalities. After the resurrection, Jesus said, "Look at my hands and my feet. It is I Myself!" Jesus called Lazarus by name when Jesus told him to come forth from his tomb, and Lazarus came forth.

Explain 1 Corinthians 15:35-39 *In this passage, our old and new bodies are compared to a seed or bulb. The shoot that is brought forth when the seed dies is a form of the old but with many new and improved qualities.*

7) Will we have memories? I think so! The rich man who went to hell remembered his brothers and asked God to send someone to warn them so they wouldn't end up where he was. How can we appreciate the absence of things like jails, crime, disease, pain, etc., in heaven unless we remember their presence on earth?

8) Will we know our loved ones in heaven, and will they know us? Surely so. This will be one of the things that will make heaven so sweet. Moses and Elijah had been dead for many years when they appeared on the Mount of Transfiguration with Jesus, and yet Peter and James and John knew who they were. Jesus was recognized by many people after his resurrection. Apparently our glorified bodies will retain enough of their former characteristics for us to be recognizable.

Randy Alcorn in his book on heaven wrote, "If you study Jesus' interactions with Mary Magdalene, Thomas, and Peter, you will see how similar they are to His interactions with these same people before He died. The fact that Jesus picked up His relationships where they had left off is a foretaste of our own lives after we are resurrected. We will experience continuity between our current lives and our resurrected lives, with the same memories and relational histories." Randy Alcorn, *Heaven* (Carol Stream, IL: Tyndale House publishers, Inc., 2004) p 117.

Our parents will still be our parents, and our children will still be our children. One of the things we look most forward to in heaven is being reunited with family and friends who have gone on before us!

I Corinthians 2:9b, *"No eye has seen, no ear has heard, no mind has conceived what God has prepared for those who love him."*

Heaven will be far greater and more wonderful than anything we could ever imagine! I wonder if there will be colors we have never seen or music notes we have never heard. Perhaps we will have more than five senses or travel through space. Who knows?

I believe we will have glorious worship services in heaven when we are finally face to face with our Lord and Savior!

I Timothy 6:17 tells us that God: "richly provides us with everything for our enjoyment." We can trust him to make heaven a wondrous place.

Song of the week: "There Will Be a Day" by Jeremy Camp